Happy As I Am

By: Devon Carrow

Illustrated by: Rachael Okula

Dedicated to everyone striving to make the world a better place.

Library of Congress Cataloging-in-Publication Data
Carrow, Devon Lucille.
Happy As I Am / Devon Carrow.

Summary: Annie learns how to love herself as she is, despite her struggles with Alopecia. [1. School – fiction. 2. Childhood – fiction   3. Bullying – fiction.]
I. Title

ISBN-13: 978-1718695122, ISBN-10: 1718695128

All illustrations by Rachael Okula.

Printed and bound in the United States of America. First printing July 2018.

Visit www.devoncarrow.com

Annie is a happy girl. She loves to dance in her princess dress, pretend she is a chef, play with her dog, and even do science experiments.

When Annie went to school for the first time, she was excited to learn, but even more excited to make friends.

However, other children made fun of Annie. She looked different than them and they did not know why. They called her mean names and this made Annie very sad.

Annie went home after school and hid in her room. She did not want to go to school anymore. She did not want other children to make fun of her because she looked different than them.

Overtime, Annie stopped doing all of the things she used to love. She did not want to dance in her princess dress or play outside with her dog... she even stopped doing science experiments.

Annie decided she would hide what made her stand out. She tried a big bow, but it would not stay still on her head. She tried a hat, but it was too itchy. Finally, Annie tried on a pink wig. It felt just right. Annie felt beautiful because she looked like all the other children at school.

Annie walked to school the next day in her new wig. She felt confident. She felt happy. She felt safe. However, as Annie opened the door, "WOOOOSH," a gust of wind blew her pink wig off.

All the children saw Annie's wig fall off. What could she do? There was nowhere to hide, no place to run, and nothing to say. But then…

As Annie started to tear up, some of her classmates realized how tough life had been for Annie and how much she tried to fit in. It was at that moment when they realized that they liked Annie not because of how her hair looked, but because of who she was and what she meant to them.

Wonderful

Beautiful Amazing

Loved  Kind

Strong Smart

funny caring

All of the children realized how brave Annie was for trying to be herself. They also realized how difficult it was for her to cover up her head. They liked that she was different. They liked how she was without the wig. Deep inside, they realized that there were things about themselves that might be different too.

Annie was a happy girl once again. She realized that she had a group of classmates who liked her for who she was. She did not have to hide the thing that made her stand out. Actually, the things that make us unique are the things that are most special about us, and that is okay. Be happy with who you are and others will be too.

What is Alopecia?

As your child may have pointed out, the character in this story, Annie, does not have any hair. Annie is based on the author, Devon, and her own experience with losing her hair due to Alopecia Areata. Alopecia is a form of hair loss that occurs when your immune system accidentally attacks your hair follicles, treating them as if they were a disease. Despite all of the research that has been done so far, scientists do not know why the immune system attacks the follicles, or how to stop it. Although it looks scary, those diagnosed with Alopecia can live healthy and happy lives.

Words to Know:

1. **Wig** - a covering for the head made of real or artificial hair
2. **Unique** - something that makes you special and distinctive
3. **Confident** - feeling happy and comfortable with yourself
4. **Bully** – a person who intentionally tries to make someone else feel bad about themselves
5. **Brave** – showing courage and strength, even if you're afraid

Topics to Discuss:

1. **What makes you unique?**
2. **What makes you confident?**
3. **What would you do if you saw someone getting bullied?**

Devon Carrow, *Author*

Devon was diagnosed with Alopecia, when she was sixteen years old. She created "The Love Spreader," an online positivity platform, with thousands of global followers, to encourage self-love, while raising Alopecia awareness. You can learn more about Devon and see upcoming projects by visiting her website www.devoncarrow.com and following "The Love Spreader" on social media.

Rachael Okula, *Illustrator*

Rachael is currently a student at Full Sail University, and is pursuing a career in the game industry as a character artist. She has a love for music, movies, and spending as much time as possible outside (unless she's in Florida, then it's hibernation time)! You can see more of her work at www.artstation.com/rachaelokula

Made in the USA
San Bernardino, CA
10 August 2018